20th CENTURY AFRICAN-AMERICAN HISTORY FOR KIDS

Readers are Leaders.
Merry, Merry
Love to all,
Aunt Claudette

20th CENTURY AFRICAN AMERICAN HISTORY FOR Kids

the MAJOR EVENTS THAT SHAPED the PAST and PRESENT

Published by Callisto Publishing LLC C/O Sourcebooks LLC
P.O. Box 4410, Naperville, Illinois 60567-4410
(630) 961-3900
callistopublishing.com

This product conforms to all applicable CPSC and CPSIA standards.

Source of Production: Wing King Tong Paper Products Co.Ltd. Shenzhen, Guangdong Province, China
Date of Production: September 2023
Run Number: 5034646

Printed and bound in China.
WKT 2

FOR MY FAVORITE YOUNG HISTORY BUFF, CARTER.

CONTENTS

INTRODUCTION

Since one of the earliest groups of enslaved Africans arrived in America in 1619, African-Americans have helped build the United States into the nation it is today. The 20th century marked a historic period of achievement for Black people and civil rights. African-Americans were finally free and trying to create their own American dream. But it wasn't easy. Freedom was much more complicated than it seemed. Laws were created to keep Black people from voting or holding public office. Other laws kept white and Black people separate. For years, Black people were treated unfairly and denied equal rights. New laws were created to protect African-Americans from unfair treatment and violence. Even then, people did not obey the laws. Civil rights leaders worked hard to make progress. African-Americans came a long way in the fight for equal rights, but there is still work to be done.

As we learn about the significant accomplishments and people of the 20th century, it's important to note the history of African-Americans. Through their contributions to art, politics, and many other fields, Black people have influenced the America we know today. This book will help you better understand how they have shaped the United States of America.

AFRICAN-AMERICANS AT THE TURN OF THE CENTURY

By the late 1890s, America was becoming a superpower in the world. But there was trouble on the home front. African-Americans were now free and trying to fend for themselves, but **racism** and inequality got in their way. In the South, **Jim Crow** laws made it illegal for Black people to work or go to school with white people. At every turn, African-Americans struggled to use the rights they were given.

The divide between the North and the South was strong. There were no Jim Crow laws in the North. In some areas, Black and white students went to school together. African-Americans went to the North in search of better opportunities. But the North wasn't the perfect place they believed it to be. Racism existed there, too.

CHAPTER ONE

1900 TO 1920

Despite many obstacles, African-Americans made great strides in the early 1900s. They organized to help those affected by racial violence, which had spread like fire throughout the South. A common form of violence was lynching, where white mobs attacked and killed a Black person. City officials and law enforcement turned a blind eye to this violence and intimidation of Black families. Black people had to protect themselves. They formed organizations and spread the word about lynching and violence. Although it was a dark time in America, there was also hope. Black people began to create a unique culture. They excelled in the arts. Black people made historic moves that defined a generation. These early achievements would serve as the beginning of a long road to equality.

NAACP founder W.E.B. Du Bois

Founding of the NAACP: 1909

In the early 1900s, white people committed ongoing violence against Black people across the country. In 1908, two Black men were held in a Springfield, Illinois, jail for alleged crimes against a white woman. The white residents wanted to take justice into their own hands. Soon a mob burned down 40 homes belonging to Springfield's Black residents. The mob vandalized Black businesses and were responsible for two deaths. But all the while, government and law officials looked the other way. Black people and allies across the nation were outraged.

In 1909, activists created the National Association for the Advancement of Colored People (NAACP) in response to the violence in Springfield. Among the founding activists were W. E. B. Du Bois and Mary Church Terrell. Du Bois was an author and a vocal activist. He and Booker T. Washington were considered the voices of African-Americans. Du Bois soon became the director of publicity and editor of the NAACP's monthly magazine, *The Crisis*.

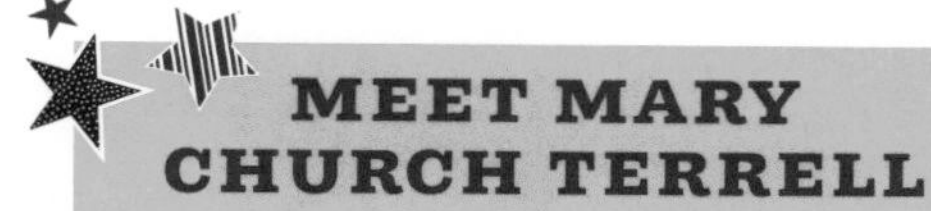

MEET MARY CHURCH TERRELL

Mary Church Terrell was an activist who fought for racial equality and women's rights during the turn of the 20th century. Terrell believed Black people could advance through education and community activism. She went on to help found the NAACP and, after winning a segregation lawsuit, became the first Black member of the American Association of University Women.

The first item on the NAACP's agenda was an anti-lynching campaign. They also fought for equal rights in voting, education, and employment opportunities for Black people. As the NAACP grew, so did their commitment to **integration**. They thought the best way to achieve equality was to end **segregation**. They financially supported civil rights cases and recruited attorneys who questioned whether segregation was constitutional. Du Bois, however, was steadily growing as a worldwide leader. His views began to shift toward a **Black nationalist** point of view. He did not think integration was the answer and instead leaned toward separate but equal. Du Bois went on to lead the NAACP into the next generation. His leadership expanded the membership of the NAACP and created a new sense of Black pride that defined African-American progress.

THE NIAGARA MOVEMENT

W. E. B. Du Bois selected a small group of influential African-American men to meet at an isolated area near Niagara Falls. All the men disagreed with Booker T. Washington's stance on race relations. They wanted to take a more assertive approach to quickly gain equality. They discussed ways to improve the lives of Black people in America. By 1906, the group had grown to 170 members. The Niagara Movement made way for the formation of the NAACP just three years later.

A man outside the UNIA headquarters

Marcus Garvey Establishes the UNIA: 1914

The NAACP promoted integration, but other growing movements did not. Jamaican-American Marcus Garvey believed in uniting Black people across the globe. This idea was called **Pan-Africanism**. Garvey did not believe integration would help Black people. He wanted them to establish a separate state.

In 1914, Garvey headed back to Jamaica and launched the Universal Negro Improvement Association (UNIA). After starting this organization, he returned to the United States to lead the charge for Pan-Africanism. Although his message of Black empowerment and separation reached many, he

MEET IDA B. WELLS

Ida B. Wells was an African-American journalist and a cofounder of the NAACP. Her work on anti-lynching campaigns in the early 1900s shed light on the growing issue of lynching throughout the South. Wells traveled internationally to discuss the lynching problem in America, even though people threatened her. Her research was important in providing evidence to support an anti-lynching bill that Black leaders promoted. Unfortunately, the bill never passed during her lifetime.

also encountered criticism. Many African-American leaders did not support him. They did not agree with his message that African-Americans should return to Africa. They also did not believe in Garvey's practice of excluding white people who wanted to help the cause. Du Bois spoke out against Garvey. He had created the NAACP with white people who wanted to fight for Black equality, too. Soon Garvey spoke against the NAACP. He felt their work to integrate the nation would hurt Black people. He didn't want Black people to **assimilate**.

Meanwhile, the Bureau of Investigations (later known as the FBI) was hot on Garvey's trail. They did not like his message of Black empowerment and saw him as a threat to society. Soon Garvey was arrested and jailed for two years. His absence affected the UNIA. They needed a strong leader, but no one could fill Garvey's shoes. The organization lost hundreds of members and never recovered. The idea of Black pride never disappeared, however. It grew in the Northern cities and attracted young people who would one day lead the movement.

BOOKER T. WASHINGTON

Booker T. Washington was a popular African-American speaker in the late 19th century. Washington believed the best way forward for African-Americans was to stay separate from white people. He also encouraged Black people to focus on self-improvement through common labor. One of his most popular ideas was that Black people should gradually earn rights from white people. This belief was vastly different from that of leaders like W. E. B. Du Bois. Du Bois felt African-Americans should demand freedom immediately.

A woman prepares to leave the South

The Great Migration: 1915

As the fight for equality continued, Black Southerners yearned for a better life. Segregation laws made job opportunities scarce. **White supremacy** made safety uncertain. In 1914, World War I began. The country needed more industrial laborers. At the time, industrial wages paid nearly three times more than the **sharecropping** or service jobs available in the South.

More than six million Black Southerners started their journey north in what would be called the **Great Migration**. Leaving the South wasn't easy. Some families had to leave their children with relatives until they had enough money to send for them in the North.

White Southerners didn't like that Black people were now able to make a living on their own.

New residents found jobs in factories and slaughterhouses. The work was dangerous, but it paid much better than work in the South. As thousands of Black families poured into Northern cities, they learned that racism existed there, too. They struggled to find housing. Building owners could legally refuse to sell or rent to them because of their race. In response, Black people began creating their own communities within cities. These communities were filled with Black businesses, arts, and education. Places like Harlem, a neighborhood in New York City, were now mostly Black.

MEET JAMES WELDON JOHNSON

James Weldon Johnson was a poet and educator. Near the end of the 19th century, as African-Americans searched for a place to fit in, Johnson wrote a poem of hope. His brother, a composer, set it to music. In 1900, the song made its debut. About 500 children performed it at the school where Johnson was principal. The song, "Lift Every Voice and Sing," went on to be a uniting cry for equality and progress.

As Black people settled into their new communities, trouble was on the horizon. Racial tensions were high and **hate crimes** were on the rise. Between 1915 and 1970, more than six million Black people had left the South for better opportunities, but they couldn't escape the shadow of racism.

BIRTH OF A NATION

***Birth of a Nation* was a 1915 silent film depicting the Ku Klux Klan, a white terrorist group, as heroes. The film made Black people look unintelligent and aggressive. Black leaders were afraid the movie would promote violence against the Black community. African-Americans protested the film and tried to get it banned. Despite their efforts, the film attracted many viewers and became a success.**

Marchers in the Silent Parade

The Silent Parade: 1917

As Black people continued to create their own communities, racial tension grew. During the summer of 1917, white residents of East St. Louis, Illinois, attacked the growing Black community and burned it to the ground. Dozens of Black people lost their lives, and thousands were left homeless. Once again, the government was silent.

The NAACP quickly organized a protest in response. On July 28, 1917, thousands of Black people marched silently along New York City's Fifth Avenue. The NAACP's call to action was "You must be in line." The organization hoped to bring attention to America's silence in the face of hate crimes against Black citizens.

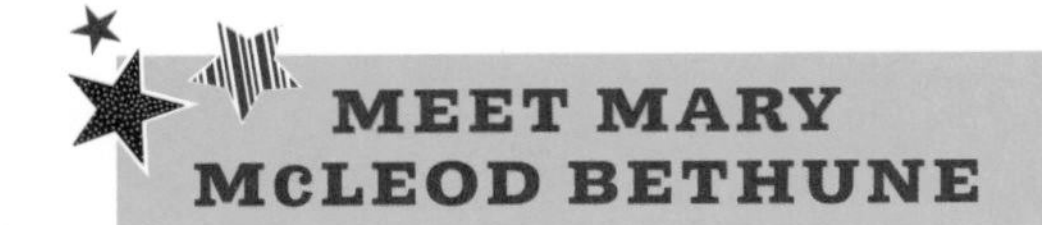

MEET MARY McLEOD BETHUNE

Mary Bethune was an activist, an educator, and a women's rights leader. She opened a training school for Black girls in the early 1900s and went on to become a noted public speaker. She was so well known and successful that wealthy white businessmen joined her organizations. Bethune made a huge impact in Florida. Her name can be found on colleges and hospitals. She also founded the National Council of Negro Women in 1935.

Men, women, and children marched to the beat of a drum. They held picket signs that explained their outrage and purpose. The signs read, "We march because we want our children to have a better life," and, "We march because we deem it a crime to be silent in the face of such barbaric acts." Children marched in front, hand in hand. The protest was silent, but the message was loud and clear. This march was the first protest of its kind in New York. It was only the second time African-Americans publicly protested for civil rights. The large attendance and growing demand for civil rights ensured it would not be the last time Black people marched for change.

NANNIE HELEN BURROUGHS

Nannie Helen Burroughs was a Black woman who fought for women's rights. She encouraged Black and white women to work together to achieve the right to vote. This goal was hard to accomplish because Black women were in a unique situation. They were **discriminated** against because they were Black *and* because they were women. Burroughs also opened the National Training School for Women and Girls to teach women skills other than domestic work.

Blues singer Bessie Smith

The Harlem Renaissance: 1918–1937

While the racial division widened, something special was happening in New York City. Harlem was quickly becoming a haven for Black people. Around 1918, a **renaissance** of Black arts and culture was underway. The Great Migration and influence from leaders like Du Bois and Garvey created a **Black Pride** movement. Du Bois led the way in ensuring that Black people excelled in creative arts. Authors like Langston Hughes, James Weldon Johnson, and Zora Neale Hurston gained popularity.

By the Twenties, Harlem was the most popular destination for Southern African-Americans. They found higher-paying jobs and better education for their children. They were also free from the violence and intimidation of the Jim Crow South. And they could finally participate in the arts. Many Black artists were able to make a living in Harlem. Black writers found that major magazines wanted to print their work. People were calling Harlem the Black Mecca, meaning it was a promised land of opportunity for Black people.

MEET MA RAINEY

Ma Rainey was an American Blues singer and recording artist. Rainey became known as the Mother of the Blues because of her influence on generations of blues singers. Rainey was popular during the height of blues music in the Twenties. She is also credited with influencing some of the Harlem Renaissance's biggest talents. Writers like Langston Hughes and Sterling Brown wrote about her.

Jazz music also became popular during this time. Southerners from New Orleans brought their sound and culture to Harlem. This sound, mixed with other Southern influences, created the musical style of jazz. In the Twenties, music venues were segregated.

But jazz music crossed the racial divide because white audiences enjoyed listening to live performances, too. Some of the famous musicians of that time were Louis Armstrong, Bessie Smith, and Duke Ellington.

The Harlem Renaissance lasted from 1918 to 1937. African-Americans were in control of how they were seen in American culture. This time period set the stage for the **civil rights movement**.

JOSEPHINE BAKER

Josephine Baker was a dancer and singer who gained popularity in Paris during the Twenties. As African-American culture and art were becoming more internationally known, Baker became famous for her performances. She also devoted her life to fighting inequality. Her goal was to have a world where everyone lived peacefully together. Baker later gave the opening remarks at the historic March on Washington in 1964 (see page 67).

Negro League pitcher Satchel Paige

Founding of the Negro National League: 1920

After the Civil War, baseball became a popular pastime. In 1876, the National League decided to keep baseball segregated. African-American players joined traveling teams instead. In 1920, Rube Foster created the Negro National League (NNL). Foster was known as one of the best pitchers of the early 1900s. He also founded and managed a successful Chicago team before starting the NNL.

Foster launched the league with eight teams. In 1923, the Eastern Colored League was formed and the two groups played each other in the World's Colored

MEET SATCHEL PAIGE

Satchel Paige was an African-American baseball pitcher whose career spanned four decades. He started in the Negro leagues, where he was known for his strong pitching. As America integrated, Paige entered the major leagues at 42 years old. He became their first Black pitcher. Paige also became the oldest new player in baseball history. He played his last game at 59 years old!

Championship until 1927. The Eastern Colored League ended in 1928, and soon afterward the **Great Depression** took its toll on the NNL. America was in a financial crisis. Many people lost their jobs, and the league could not afford to stay open. It seemed that baseball for African-Americans would be unattainable. Five years later, Gus Greenlee restarted the Negro National League. He was an African-American businessman who had managed several successful enterprises, including all-star baseball games. The NNL's annual all-star games went on to attract more than 500,000 fans.

The Black baseball players were known for their speed and showmanship. They began to attract the attention of white recruiters. There was talk that baseball would soon integrate. Integration was a good thing, but it also meant that there would no longer be a need for the NNL. As the possibility grew stronger, Black athletes had to consider how they would fit into a world that had previously excluded them.

KATHERINE DUNHAM AND THE NEGRO DANCE GROUP

While Black men advanced during the integration of sports, Black women were also making strides. Katherine Dunham was an African-American dancer who traveled to the Caribbean to learn new dance styles. She was also an anthropologist, or a person who studies culture. She wrote about the people of Haiti and their performing styles. Dunham opened a Black dance school, where she trained young dancers in diverse dance styles. She created the first Black modern dance company in 1930.

CHAPTER TWO

1921 TO 1940

America changed during the Twenties. Booming economic growth allowed more people to buy cars and created a new generation of wealth. African-Americans found opportunities in the North and found fame in the North's new interest in Black culture, arts, and music.

But 10 years later, the economic boom was over. The Great Depression took hold between 1929 and 1940. As Americans struggled with job loss and economic hardships, African-Americans were hit with many more obstacles. Black people were the first to see jobs cut and experienced the highest unemployment rate. Across the nation, Black families dealt with a new wave of violent attacks and racial unrest. Segregated Black communities were no longer secure havens. Segregation was still in effect. Within the decade, Harlem's Black Renaissance was over. It was a time of great sorrow. Despite the uptick of violence and poverty, however, African-Americans uncovered a new sense of pride and courage. The dream of racial equality and justice was just on the horizon.

Aftermath of the Tulsa Race Massacre

The Tulsa Race Massacre: 1921

Tulsa, Oklahoma, was a bustling and wealthy city in the Twenties. It was also very segregated and known for its **vigilante justice**. Tulsa's 10,000 Black residents lived in the Greenwood District. This successful business area was known as Black Wall Street because of its booming businesses and prosperous residents.

On May 30, 1921, a Black teenager named Dick Rowland was arrested. He had entered an elevator run by a white woman. The white woman screamed, and Rowland ran away. Rumors spread that the boy had harmed the woman. Soon an angry white mob gathered at the courthouse demanding that the sheriff hand over the young man. A group of Black men were also there to protect Rowland. The groups clashed, and chaos followed. Over the next few hours, thousands of white residents invaded the Greenwood District. Some were from neighboring towns. They looted and burned down the homes and businesses. By the next day, the historic neighborhood was destroyed. Ash and smoke were all that remained. Black families had nowhere to go. Many Black residents were unjustly imprisoned, and there were hundreds of deaths.

MEET O. W. GURLEY

O. W. Gurley was an entrepreneur who had worked as a teacher and postal worker. He moved to the Tulsa area during the oil boom. He bought 40 acres of land in 1905. The area would eventually be known as Greenwood. Here, he owned a store and sold his land to homeowners. When the Tulsa Race Massacre occurred, Gurley lost everything and had to flee from his home.

Hours after the massacre, also known as the Tulsa Race Riots, charges against Rowland were dropped. The police concluded that he had committed no crime. But the damage was done. Historians estimate that hundreds of Black residents were killed. The once-bustling, bright community was gone. The surviving Black residents were forced to move to other areas in search of safety. The massacre was quickly covered up, but the survivors kept their story and the history of Greenwood District alive.

BLACK WALL STREET

The Greenwood District was one of the wealthiest African-American communities in the nation during the early 20th century. Greenwood Avenue was known as Black Wall Street because of its luxury shops, restaurants, businesses, and movie theater. Black Wall Street was built by and for Black people who wanted to escape segregation and racial injustice.

Pullman porter Alfred MacMillan

The Pullman Porters Union: 1925

As the 20th century progressed, many African-American men found jobs as porters on railroad sleeping cars, or trains. The porters carried passengers' bags, shined their shoes, cleaned up, and served passengers. Porters were extremely overworked, often working 400 hours a month! George Pullman, who ran the Pullman Company, hired thousands of African-Americans—many of them formerly enslaved people—for these positions. He reasoned that Black workers would take low-paying jobs and endure racism. The company soon became the largest employer of Black men in the country.

MEET A. PHILIP RANDOLPH

Asa Philip Randolph was an influential civil rights leader and union organizer. Before taking on the Pullman Company, he had organized Black workers in the early 1900s. He even founded a magazine, *The Messenger*, that focused on rights for Black laborers. He went on to lead several successful protests and work with leaders during the historic March on Washington in 1964 (see page 67). Randolph's victories helped shape African-American history.

As the popularity of the luxurious sleeping cars grew, A. Philip Randolph, a social activist, noticed that members of the American Federal Labor union were treated fairly. The union helped its railway workers get better pay, hours, and treatment—but only white workers. Randolph knew that organizing and standing together was the only chance for the Black workers to be treated fairly. He formed a union for the Black workers called the Brotherhood of Sleeping Car Porters (BSCP). They asked for higher wages and fewer hours.

But the Pullman Company didn't want to pay the Black workers more money, even though they were the worst paid of all railroad workers. The company also didn't want to decrease their hours. Pullman fought against every attempt to compel them to treat their Black workers fairly. It took more than a decade before the BSCP and Pullman came to an agreement. Finally, they agreed that porters would receive a pay raise and set a limit of 240 working hours per month. This agreement was a massive accomplishment. Randolph secured the first-ever contract between a Black union and a major company. Other Black organizations and leaders took note. The union's success was a blueprint for organizing groups to fight for equality.

BLACK PORTERS

Black porters are a significant part of African-American history. Although they endured racism and were underpaid, these workers were a major part of the Great Migration that saw Black families move north. They also helped shape the Black middle class, as their pay often afforded them escape from the widespread poverty in the South.

Negro History Week poster

The First Negro History Week: 1926

As African-Americans continued to prosper in the Twenties, Dr. Carter G. Woodson wanted to do more to honor Black heritage. He had already formed the Association for the Study of Negro Life and History (ASNLH), which focused on researching Black history. Woodson was dedicated to promoting the importance of Black history. He asked his **fraternity** brothers to help him spread the message. Woodson was a member of Omega Psi Phi, one of the nine fraternities and sororities established for college-educated Black people (see Historically Black Colleges and Universities, page 38). The fraternity created Negro History and

Literature Week in 1924. It was a great first step in showcasing the importance of Black achievement in America. But Woodson was on a mission to make Black history a bigger celebration. He announced Negro History Week in February 1926. He chose February because both President Abraham Lincoln and Frederick Douglass, a former enslaved person turned abolitionist, were born in that month. Lincoln was popular with African-Americans because of the **Emancipation Proclamation**. Douglass Day was celebrated on February 14, Douglass's birthday. It wasn't nationally known but had been growing in popularity since the 1900s. Woodson thought Negro

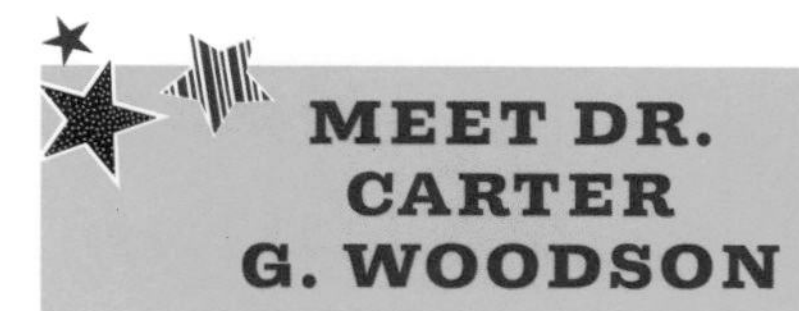

MEET DR. CARTER G. WOODSON

The son of former enslaved people, Carter G. Woodson was the second Black man to receive a PhD from Harvard University. As a historian, he struggled to fit into the mostly white field. Woodson wanted to create a place for the study of Black history. He knew if he didn't, no one else would. Woodson began by researching African-American culture. He wrote about the Black church, slavery, and migration. His research became the basis for African-American appreciation.

History Week would expand the celebrations of these two important figures. He also wanted to encourage Americans to have a greater appreciation for the history of Black people in America.

Negro History Week was more than just a name. Woodson's team provided teaching materials so people could learn about important dates and historical figures. Although it was initially a Black movement, some white schools were learning the history, too. Woodson's vision started small but continued to progress. Today, Black History Month is nationally recognized and celebrated for the entire month of February. Woodson's vision encouraged generations to take pride in their history.

THE DIVINE NINE

The National Pan-Hellenic Council, sometimes called the Divine Nine, represents the nine organizations of Black sororities and fraternities. These organizations were founded during a time when Black students were not allowed to join white fraternities and sororities. These groups boast some of the most well-known figures in African-American history, like Dr. Martin Luther King Jr. and Vice President Kamala Harris.

The Scottsboro Boys in a Jefferson County jail

The Trial of the Scottsboro Boys: 1931

By the Thirties, the years of economic growth were over. The nation was now in the grip of the Great Depression. During this time, many unemployed Americans, Black and white, hitched rides on freight trains to search for jobs around the country. On March 25, 1931, a fight broke out in a freight train in Alabama. Police arrested nine Black teenagers. The youngest was just 13 years old. Things soon took a turn for the worse. Two white women accused the boys of committing a horrible crime aboard the train. The teenagers were transferred to an Alabama jail. A white mob surrounded the jail. They didn't care about what had really happened; they just wanted revenge. The Black people in the area had likely heard about the massacre in Tulsa. They feared that the mob would hurt not only the boys but also any other Black people they encountered.

MEET ROY WRIGHT

Leroy "Roy" Wright was the youngest of the Scottsboro Boys. He was only 13 when he was arrested. Wright had traveled to Alabama with his brother Andrew in search of work. Andrew was arrested as well. During Roy's trial, 11 jurors voted for the death penalty. Only one juror voted for life in prison. The split helped Roy. He avoided the death penalty but went on to spend six years in prison. In 1937, he was released.

The nine teenagers became known as the Scottsboro Boys. They went to trial in April 1931 and were sentenced to death. The International Labor Defense (ILD) took the boys' case and filed an **appeal**. The ILD led a campaign to help free all nine boys. The Alabama Supreme Court, however, upheld the previous sentence. The young men were once again facing death.

The US Supreme Court ruled that the group had been denied the right to counsel, or proper defense in court. The justices agreed that the boys' Fourteenth

Amendment right, which gave Black people equal protection under the law, had been violated. It was a landmark decision that gave everyone the right to a proper lawyer. The Scottsboro Boys went back to court. They had evidence that proved they were innocent. One of the women who had accused them changed her story and even agreed to help them. Still, another all-white jury recommended the death penalty.

Years later, the US Supreme Court overturned the guilty verdicts. They ruled it was not fair that the jury excluded Black people. This decision helped integrate future juries. The Scottsboro Boys' trials gained international attention. Eventually, all the young men were pardoned, but some did not live to see their names cleared.

THE CENTRAL PARK FIVE

Similar to the Scottsboro Boys case, in 1989, five teenagers were accused of a crime against a white woman. The oldest boy in the case was just 16. The trial received national attention. Eventually all five were found innocent. Most spent several years in prison, however, and faced unfair treatment.

Tuskegee Institute workers

The Tuskegee Experiments: 1932

While the Scottsboro Boys were fighting for their lives, down the road, another group of Black men were facing a different kind of prejudice. In 1932, Black men in rural Alabama were mostly sharecroppers. Many had never been to a doctor. When the United States Public Health Service announced a medical study that promised free health care, 600 African-American men signed up. Many of these men had a disease called syphilis. The Public Health Service wanted to study the progression of the disease.

The men were not told what disease they had. Instead, doctors said they were being treated for "bad blood," a term that was used in that area to refer to different illnesses. The sick men were also told they were being treated, but they were not. Instead, the health workers gave them placebos, or fake treatments. Without proper treatment for syphilis, some of the men went blind or experienced severe mental illness. Some experienced other health problems. Others died.

MEET THE TUSKEGEE INSTITUTE

The Tuskegee Institute was founded in 1881 by Booker T. Washington to train Black teachers. Washington promoted economic self-reliance. He eventually introduced trades and agricultural skills as class options. In the Twenties, the school became strictly academic. Black students could earn a degree just like white students. But eventually the institute became home to experimental treatments on local Black farmers. Still, it was an important place in the history of Black education in America.

During the trial, a simple cure for syphilis was discovered: a drug called penicillin. But as the experiment went on, researchers refused to give the men this medicine. By that time more than 100 men had died of the disease or related issues. Syphilis also affected families. The men had passed on the disease to their wives and even their newborn babies. It wasn't until the Seventies that the experiments were uncovered. The survivors and the relatives of those who died received money from the government. But the effects of the horrible experiment were long-lasting. Many African-Americans did not trust government health officials. They feared that what happened in Tuskegee could happen again. African-Americans felt unprotected by the government. They needed something to believe in and someone to be a light in an otherwise dark time in American history.

HISTORICALLY BLACK COLLEGES AND UNIVERSITIES

Known as HBCUs, these colleges and universities were founded when Black people were not allowed to enroll in white schools. The first HBCU was started in 1837. Today, HBCUs are spread around the nation. They continue to provide excellent education with a strong sense of Black culture.

Jesse Owens at the Berlin Olympics

The Berlin Olympics: 1936

While the world dealt with the effects of the Great Depression, Germany was becoming a superpower. After its defeat in World War I, Germany was given the chance to host the 1936 Summer Olympics in Berlin. Many thought it was an opportunity for Germany to make a positive statement. No one suspected Adolf Hitler, a dictator, would change the world. Hitler was excited to host the Olympics and wanted to show that the "Aryan race," a supposed group of white people who looked a certain way, was superior to all other races. Hitler made sure all the athletes who represented Germany in the Olympics were Aryan.

MEET ALICE COACHMAN

Jesse Owens was not the only Olympian to break racial barriers. During the 1948 Olympics, Alice Coachman became the first Black woman to win an Olympic gold medal. Coachman was a star track and field athlete at the Tuskegee Institute. She went on to compete with great runners from around the world. Coachman was the only American woman to win any medal that year.

A total of 49 nations sent around 4,000 athletes to compete in the Summer Olympics. Track and field was a popular event. Twenty-three-year-old Jesse Owens was one of four African-Americans competing in track and field. He was surrounded by hateful signs and clear racism in Nazi Germany. Despite the harsh environment, Owens became the star of the Olympics. He tied the world record in the 100-meter race and broke the world records in the 200-meter race and the broad jump. He also won first place as a member of a 4 x 100 relay team. Owens was unstoppable. His record-breaking achievement was a great win for America. It also disproved Hitler's theory that the Aryan race was superior. Most important, Owens's win was special to African-Americans.

He proved African-Americans could not only compete but also prevail against the hardships of racism. Although Owens didn't continue racing, his achievements were the benchmark for integrating African-Americans in sports.

OWENS'S RETURN TO AMERICA

Jesse Owens left Germany as an international star. Not only had he won a gold medal, but he also disproved Hitler's theory of white supremacy. When Owens came back to America, however, he did not receive a hero's welcome. White Olympic medalists were applauded for their achievement. They came back to a proud and welcoming America. Owens returned to the same racial issues as before.

CHAPTER THREE

1941 TO 1960

As a new decade began, America was in a crisis. The country was slowly climbing out of the shadows of the Great Depression. A new war had begun. Germany, Italy, and Japan had joined together to become the Axis powers. They launched a war against Great Britain, France, and Russia, who were called the Allied forces. By the end of 1941, America entered World War II with the Allies after Japan attacked American soil at Pearl Harbor, Hawaii. Men quickly lined up to serve their country.

With many of the men gone, there were no industrial workers for defense plants or factories. For the first time, women took industry jobs once reserved for men. America and its allies eventually won the war. But for African-Americans, the war overseas and the war at home were very similar. African-Americans saw the world come together to defeat an evil enemy and restore equality and peace. They saw the world defeat prejudice and denounce discrimination. But they did not see that same defeat in America, their own country. African-American soldiers still came home to segregation and racial injustice. But the new generation of African-Americans had seen how organizations demanded change. They had learned more about their own history and were better educated than their parents. They knew change would not come unless they demanded it.

Jackie Robinson

Jackie Robinson Breaks the Color Barrier: 1947

In 1947, the popularity of the Negro leagues had faded. Baseball was still a popular pastime, but Black players could not play on the same teams as white players. Years earlier, America rooted for Jesse Owens as he led his team of Black and white runners to victory. The message was clear: Black players could perform. Branch Rickey, general manager of the Dodgers baseball team, had his eye on the Negro leagues. He thought it was time that the sport was integrated. He saw promise in a young Jackie Robinson.

Jackie Robinson had played with the Negro leagues and was a standout athlete in college. After a few practices, Rickey offered him a contract. Playing for the Dodgers wasn't just a regular job; Robinson would be the first Black player in Major League Baseball. Also, baseball fans were known for being rowdy. Rickey knew the fans would not want Robinson to play. He asked Robinson not to react when confronted with racism. Robinson agreed, but it was no small task.

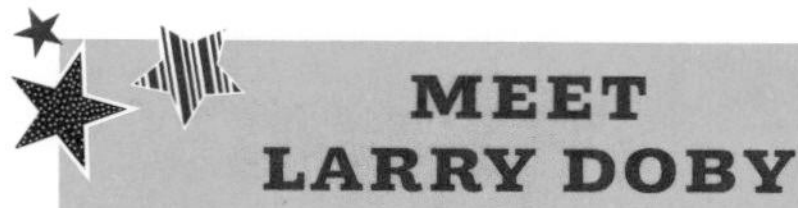

MEET LARRY DOBY

Jackie Robinson is known as the first African-American to play for Major League Baseball. But just a few months later, Larry Doby became the second to integrate the sport by breaking the color barrier for the American League. Doby played in Cleveland. He first played in the Negro leagues and helped his team win the Negro League World Series. From there, he went directly to the major leagues.

On April 15, 1947, Robinson stepped into history. He became the first African-American baseball player for the major leagues. Not everyone was happy about his achievement. Some of his teammates were rude to him and didn't want him on the team. Crowds jeered at him, and some even threw things. Robinson didn't say anything. He continued to play and kept his promise not to fight back. Eventually Robinson's great athleticism won over his critics. He helped his team win and even get to the World Series. After proving himself, Robinson became vocal about equal rights. He hoped that speaking out would help other African-Americans. His success showed that integration was possible. If sports could integrate, what about schools? What would be next? By breaking the color barrier, Robinson put African-Americans a step closer to achieving equality.

JACKIE ROBINSON DAY

On April 15, Major League Baseball honors the day Jackie Robinson made his league debut. On that day, all players and coaches wear Robinson's uniform number, 42, to mark the end of segregation in baseball.

Tuskegee Airmen

Integration of the US Armed Forces: 1948

African-Americans had served in the military since the American Revolution. They served separately from whites, however, and often faced mistreatment. The Tuskegee Airmen were a group of African-Americans who had completed training to become pilots. They proved themselves in combat and served alongside white pilots. As World War II came to an end, white soldiers returned as war heroes. They were celebrated for their bravery.

But African-American soldiers came home to racist attacks and poor treatment. In South Carolina, one veteran was attacked and beaten just days after returning from war. There was a series of beatings and murders of recently returned Black veterans in the South. Black civil rights groups took action. A. Philip Randolph, the civil rights leader behind the Pullman Porters Union, led the charge. He wanted the military to integrate. Randolph put pressure on President Harry Truman to act. He threatened that Black men would boycott the military altogether if the president didn't do something immediately.

On July 26, 1948, President Truman signed Executive Order 9981. The order desegregated the US Armed Forces. It was a major achievement for the civil rights movement.

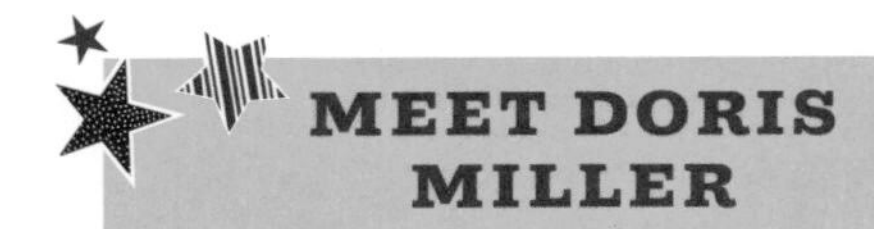

MEET DORIS MILLER

Before the armed forces were integrated, Black soldiers worked as cooks and janitors. Doris Miller was a Navy cook. During the Japanese attack on Pearl Harbor, Miller went into action. He had never been trained to use weapons, but he shot down Japanese planes. He also carried wounded sailors to safety. For his bravery, Miller was awarded the Navy Cross, which is the second-highest military honor.

Not everyone welcomed the change. Some military leaders did not agree with Truman. Others were unsure of how soldiers would react to integration. It took six years to fully desegregate the armed forces. Once again, integration was at the forefront of the news. It seemed like things were changing for the better. Black people saw they had the power to demand change.

THE TUSKEGEE AIRMEN

In the late Thirties, a war was coming and America needed more pilots. President Franklin Roosevelt announced a program to train Black pilots in Tuskegee, Alabama. Black men from across the nation joined. A group called the Tuskegee Airmen was born. These men led nearly 200 successful missions. They escorted heavy bombers and shot down enemy planes. The tails of their planes were painted red, which earned them the nickname "Red Tails." They proved that African-Americans could do well in aerial combat.

Little Rock Nine member Elizabeth Eckford

Brown v. Board of Education: 1954

In 1896, the US Supreme Court passed a major decision that became known as "separate but equal." This idea held that it was legal to keep people segregated by skin color as long as their separate facilities were equal. In reality, however, facilities like schools, restrooms, and train cars for Black people were of much poorer quality than those for white people.

In 1952, Oliver Brown sued the Topeka School Board for barring his daughter from entering a local school because of her race. Soon the NAACP took the case to the Supreme Court. The courts combined the

Brown case and four other cases that dealt with segregation into one case called *Brown v. Board of Education of Topeka*.

Thurgood Marshall led the team of NAACP attorneys in challenging the 1896 ruling that made segregation legal. At the end of his argument, Marshall said the only way the court could uphold segregation was if they believed Black people were inferior to white people. It was a strong statement. The justices took weeks to make a decision. Finally, on May 17, 1954, the court ruled that separate but equal was unconstitutional and that public schools must integrate.

It was an important win, but integrating schools was not easy. In 1957, nine Black teenagers tried to integrate a high school in Little Rock, Arkansas.

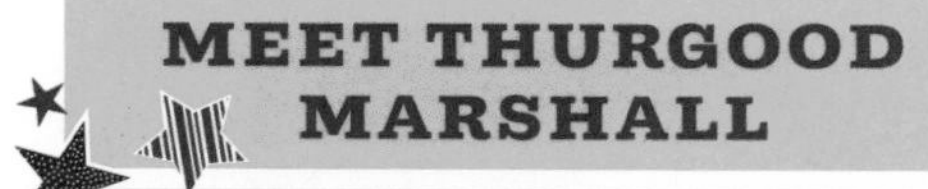

MEET THURGOOD MARSHALL

Thurgood Marshall went to law school at Howard University, a historically Black college. Shortly afterward, he became lead staff attorney for the NAACP. Throughout his career, he won an impressive 29 of the 32 cases he argued before the Supreme Court. His greatest victory was *Brown v. Board of Education*. Marshall also made history as the first African-American Supreme Court Justice in 1967.

They were met by angry mobs who called them names and threw things at them. President Dwight Eisenhower sent the National Guard to help them enter the school. Six years after the court's decision, Ruby Bridges had to be escorted by US Marshals for an entire year to attend a New Orleans school. She became the first Black student to integrate an elementary school in the South. The *Brown v. Board of Education* decision helped spark the civil rights movement. Although it would take years for Black people to be treated fairly, this historic win was one in a series of victories for Black people across the nation.

RUBY BRIDGES

Many areas of the South refused to change despite being ordered to do so by the Supreme Court. On November 14, 1960, Ruby Bridges was escorted to an elementary school by US Marshals. People threw things and shouted at her, but she continued to walk. At just six years old, Bridges became the first Black child to desegregate an all-white Louisiana school.

Civil rights activist Rosa Parks

The Montgomery Bus Boycott: 1955

A year after *Brown v. Board of Education*, America was still divided. The South held on to its Jim Crow laws while civil rights groups pushed for more justice. In Montgomery, Alabama, Black people were still required to sit at the back of buses. They also had to give up their seats to white riders if the white section up front was full.

Rosa Parks, a local woman, refused to give up her seat when asked. She was arrested and fined. Soon civil rights groups organized and called for a boycott. They asked Montgomery's Black residents to stop riding the bus until the city agreed to desegregate the bus system.

MEET JO ANN ROBINSON

Jo Ann Robinson was an activist who helped during the Montgomery Bus Boycott. She was a leader in the Montgomery Women's Political Council (WPC). This group was dedicated to improving African-Americans' status in America. When Rosa Parks was arrested, Robinson went into action. She was ready to lead a boycott that would pressure the city to end segregation on buses. Her efforts with the WPC led to widespread support of the boycott.

African-Americans across Montgomery supported the plan. Forty thousand Black bus riders boycotted the bus system on December 5. They created a system for carpooling or walking in groups. Black taxi drivers charged less so people could afford to ride. Meanwhile, Black leaders formed a new organization called the Montgomery Improvement Association. The organization elected a young pastor named Martin Luther King Jr. He and other leaders pushed to get rid of the segregation laws. The city resisted. But Black riders accounted for about 75 percent of their customers. The city was losing more money every day.

Finally, the Montgomery court ruled that segregation on buses was unconstitutional. This decision didn't stop city officials. They appealed the rule, but the Supreme Court agreed with the Montgomery court. Segregation on Montgomery buses ended on December 21, 1956. The Montgomery Bus Boycott had lasted more than a year. Its success put King in the spotlight. He quickly became a leader of the civil rights movement.

The success also brought problems. Black bus riders were attacked and even shot at. Later, Black churches were bombed, killing innocent people, including children. Authorities also found a bomb at King's home. But the boycott proved that African-Americans had strength in numbers. Parks and King inspired African-Americans across the nation. The nonviolent message sparked a new wave of protests.

CLAUDETTE COLVIN

Months before Rosa Parks's bold action, 15-year-old Claudette Colvin refused to give up her seat to a white woman on a segregated bus. She was arrested and eventually went to court to challenge the segregation rule. Colvin's act was not widely publicized, but it set the stage for Parks and other nonviolent protesters.

Motown group The Velvelettes

Founding of Motown Records: 1959

Black music and culture has always been at the forefront of American history. From the humble beginnings of jazz and blues, Black people contributed to many forms of art. They didn't always own the rights to their creations, however.

Berry Gordy Jr. was a Black music store owner who had a passion for music. He started his career writing songs, then producing. He created Tamla Records to produce and write more chart-topping songs by Black artists. He later renamed the company Motown Records as a tribute to Detroit, which was called "motor town" because of its large automobile industry. Motown became a hit. In less than 10 years, the record company had made more than $20 million.

But Motown was not just a record label. Berry Gordy Jr. was the only Black person to own a multimillion-dollar music company. He brought out many acts and singers who went on to make history. Gordy created a lane for Black music that was totally produced by a Black person. No one else had ever done it.

MEET THE MOTOWN SOUND

Motown was known for its soul music with a pop appeal. Audiences could recognize a Motown record by a few key characteristics. The Motown sound used tambourines, a bass guitar, and call-and-response singing style. Call-and-response is an African-American tradition from gospel music where the singer sings, or calls out, and the audience responds. The Motown sound combined gospel traditions, soul, and popular beats to create the historic music we still enjoy today.

The Motown sound took over the radio waves and flooded people's homes. Listeners across the world got to know the Motown artists. Gordy was able to use music to integrate households. As Black music gained popularity, Americans of all races saw Black artists on TV and even in concerts. Music was breaking down the color barriers. The civil rights movement was underway and the Motown sound was the tempo of the movement.

THE WHITEWASHING OF BLACK MUSIC

Beginning in the Fifties, many rock 'n' roll artists became legends. Many of their hits, however, were originally written and performed by Black artists. In some cases, the white artists recorded the song and gained money and fame from it. The original Black artists did not receive credit.

Sit-in at a Woolworth's lunch counter

The Greensboro Lunch Counter Sit-Ins: 1960

The Sixties marked a time of significant change. As the decade began, young people took the reins. In Greensboro, North Carolina, four Black college students were denied service at a lunch counter in a department store. They decided to sit in as a protest. Influenced by nonviolent protests, the young men wanted to make a statement. They stayed at the counter, refusing to leave, until the store closed. The next day, more students joined the sit-in. This movement spread to other college campuses throughout the nation. The message

MEET DIANE NASH

Diane Nash was a civil rights leader and SNCC organizer. The violence surrounding the Freedom Rides made many people nervous. Bus drivers soon stopped offering to drive protesters to the Deep South, which caused an abrupt stop to the movement. Nash then recruited a small group of students to continue, despite the looming threat of violence and possible death. She went on to become an icon in the civil rights movement.

was clear: We will not be moved. Young Black and white people joined in peaceful protest against segregation in all areas. They sat in at libraries, beaches, and even hotels.

Within months, the movement had spread to 55 cities across 13 states. National media coverage brought more attention to the protests and the civil rights movement. By the summer of 1960, lunch counters and other eating facilities across the South were integrated.

The sit-in influenced another group, the Student Nonviolent Coordinating Committee (SNCC). They began leading civil rights protests and organized Freedom Rides throughout the South. The Freedom Rides bused Black and white people through the South to protest segregated bus terminals, restaurants, and more. The Sixties were a turning point in Black history. The fight for civil rights had finally made it to the international stage. The lunch-counter protests were just the beginning.

THE GREENSBORO FOUR

The four students who started the sit-ins in Greensboro were Joseph McNeil, Franklin McCain, David Richmond, and Jibreel Khazan. They became known as the Greensboro Four. Although other sit-ins had taken place, this one was different. The young men did not have the backing of large organizations like the NAACP. They made a plan and carried it out alone. Their act sparked a new movement for young activists.

CHAPTER FOUR

1961 TO 1980

As the civil rights movement gained steam, African-Americans were on the cusp of change. The last decade proved that change was possible. Voting rights were protected and schools had to open their doors for all students. Integration changed the face of America. But the fight was not over. Nonviolent protests were met with extreme violence. People around the world saw the ugliness of injustice on their television sets. They saw Black children sprayed with fire hoses and attacked by dogs. They saw peaceful marches end in violence against those marching. As the violence worsened, peaceful leaders and even children were killed.

The assassination of African-American leaders left a stain on the movement's progress. The generation of nonviolent protesters birthed a fierce new movement. The new generation of changemakers did not follow the nonviolent methods of past leaders. They wanted immediate change, and they fought to protect their communities. This movement stemmed from pride and protection but met an untimely fate. Change had finally arrived. But it hadn't come easily. The next two decades would be the most important years in the fight for freedom.

Martin Luther King Jr. in the Birmingham Jail

The Birmingham Campaign: 1963

Martin Luther King Jr. was quickly becoming the face of the civil rights movement. Despite the positive changes in recent years, King felt it was time to push harder for more rights. He and his organization, the Southern Christian Leadership Conference (SCLC), met with a local movement in Birmingham, Alabama. At the time, Birmingham was one of the most segregated cities in the nation. It was the perfect place to stage a peaceful campaign against segregation. They planned multiple **demonstrations** to get national attention. On April 3, 1963, the campaign launched. It included lunch counter sit-ins, a march to city hall, and a boycott of white merchants. More and more people volunteered, and soon there were kneel-ins at church, sit-ins at the library, and a march to register voters. Birmingham officials were angry. They quickly passed laws against protests. But that didn't stop the protesters. Many were arrested. King knew it was time for another push.

MEET FRED SHUTTLESWORTH

Fred Shuttlesworth was a civil rights activist who co-founded the Southern Christian Leadership Conference. He was a minister in Birmingham who worked closely with Martin Luther King Jr. during the 1963 Birmingham Campaign. He also helped organize the Freedom Rides. Shuttlesworth took in Freedom Riders after violent attacks. He was known as a forgiving man who fought for equal rights.

On April 12, King was arrested for protesting. He knew his arrest would cause a national debate because of his popularity. Many people had opinions about King going to jail. Some of the local religious leaders did not approve of King's action. They felt that African-Americans should wait for justice instead of acting. King was disappointed. He wrote a letter to them, explaining that no one should have to keep waiting for someone else to do the right thing. His "Letter from a Birmingham Jail" was eventually published all over the world. King gained more supporters and was released from jail a few days later.

Days later another leader made a drastic decision. SCLC organizer James Bevel decided to use young people to protest. No one had ever tried this tactic. Beginning on May 2, more than 1,000 Black children as young as elementary schoolers tried to march into downtown Birmingham. Over a period of days, a large number of police officers was sent to stop them. The nation watched in horror as police eventually used high-powered hoses and attack dogs, injuring many children. It was called the Children's Crusade. Sadly, nonviolent protests would continue to be met with violence.

FREEDOM RIDERS

The Freedom Riders were young activists who traveled through the Deep South protesting segregated bus terminals. They were met with horrible violence at many stops. John Lewis, who would become a civil rights leader, was one of the original 13 Freedom Riders.

Protesters at the March on Washington

The March on Washington and the Civil Rights Act of 1964

After a battle in Birmingham, King and other civil rights leaders set their eyes on a national march to end injustice. A. Philip Randolph and Bayard Rustin were the top African-American organizers. Randolph had led the Pullman Porters Union (see page 27). Rustin had helped organize the Freedom Riders (see page 66). Together they planned the national March on Washington for Jobs and Freedom. They asked John Lewis and the SNCC to participate. The NAACP also joined.

MEET DAISY BATES

Daisy Bates was a civil rights activist and journalist. She spent her early years in a foster home after her mother was murdered by three white men. Her mother's death made her want to fight for justice. She and her husband started a newspaper in Arkansas called *The Arkansas State Press*. It was the only Black newspaper covering civil rights issues. Bates also led the NAACP during the Fifties. She later gave a speech during the March on Washington.

President John F. Kennedy was concerned the march would end in violence. He met with the leaders. Randolph, King, and the others insisted it was the right time to protest. Eventually the president supported the march. On August 28, 1963, more than 250,000 people gathered at the Lincoln Memorial for the March on Washington.

Randolph was the first speaker. Other speakers included John Lewis, Josephine Baker, and activist Daisy Bates. Performers Marian Anderson, Bob Dylan, and Mahalia Jackson attended, too. Finally, King took the podium to deliver a short speech. But as he was speaking, Jackson called out for him to tell the audience about his dream of equality for all.

King changed his speech. He put aside his notes and spoke for 16 minutes! After each line, King repeated, "I have a dream."

The march was a success. But change had not happened overnight. On September 15, a Black church was bombed. The explosion killed four Black girls. The nation was in shock. In November, President Kennedy was assassinated. On July 2, 1964, President Lyndon Johnson signed the **Civil Rights Act of 1964**. This act made it illegal to discriminate against someone at work because of their race, color, religion, sex, or national origin. With the help of the March on Washington, justice had arrived. But so many had been hurt in the struggle for freedom.

FOUR LITTLE GIRLS

On September 15, 1963, white terrorists bombed the 16th Street Baptist Church in Birmingham. They wanted to send a message to the Black community to stop demonstrating for civil rights. The explosion killed four African-American girls: Addie Mae Collins, Cynthia Wesley, Carole Robertson, and Carol Denise McNair. It also injured many others. For years the FBI and local communities knew that the Ku Klux Klan was behind the attack, but nobody was tried for the crime until 1977.

Protesters marching from Selma to Montgomery

Bloody Sunday and the Voting Rights Act: 1965

Back in Alabama, things were heating up. The Civil Rights Act of 1964 had little effect on how African-Americans were treated there. In Dallas County, Alabama, African-Americans were more than half the population but only 2 percent of registered voters. Black voters were discouraged from registering. Leaders from the SNCC and NAACP planned a march in Selma in support of Black voting rights. A few days before the march, Jimmie Lee Jackson, an activist, was killed by a state trooper in Marion, Alabama. It was a devastating blow to King and the other marchers, but they decided to go on.

John Lewis led 600 peaceful marchers across the Edmund Pettus Bridge in Selma. But when they tried to cross, they were met by state police. Chaos erupted as the police began pushing them back. The marchers were beaten with clubs and trampled by dogs. The police threw tear gas at them. Many people were hurt. The news covered the march, and people across the nation were again horrified by what they saw. Hundreds of people from across the United States volunteered to join the protest.

MEET THE NATION OF ISLAM

The Nation of Islam (NOI) rose to power during the Sixties. This religious organization was founded by Wallace Fard Muhammad in 1930. They preached that Black families should separate themselves from white people. They also called for a separate state for Black people. The message appealed to Black families who were tired of mistreatment and ready to be in control of their own lives. Malcolm X, a leader in the nation, was the most popular speaker. By 1963, it is estimated that more than 10,000 people were members of the NOI. Malcolm X was assassinated in 1965.

After two more tries, the protesters finally crossed the bridge. By that time, they had protection from both the FBI and the Alabama National Guard. They crossed the bridge, but it cost lives. During the second attempt, a young minister named James Reeb was killed by a white mob. The deaths of two activists and the footage of police attacking unarmed protesters swayed public opinion. Many American citizens wanted something done quickly. On August 6, 1965, President Johnson signed the **Voting Rights Act of 1965**. It made it illegal to harass, threaten, or prevent someone from voting. Lewis, King, and other leaders had won a long, hard fight.

ST. AUGUSTINE PROTESTS

Nearly 10 years after the *Brown v. Board* decision, officials of St. Augustine, Florida, still refused to desegregate the city. In late 1963, locals and Northern allies began protesting. They eventually called in the Southern Christian Leadership Conference to help. After nearly a year, the city desgregated. This movement helped to pass the Civil Rights Bill of 1964.

Malcolm X, a leader who influenced the Black Power movement

The Rise of the Black Power Movement: 1966

While King and others preached a nonviolent method of change, a new movement was getting started in Oakland, California. Huey Newton and Bobby Seale were students at Merritt College. They formed the Negro History Fact Group to call on their school to offer Black History classes. They did not like how classes ignored contributions by African-Americans. Newton and Seale were influenced by the teachings of Malcolm X. He taught that Black people should seek freedom "by any means necessary."

After the assassination of Malcolm X and the death of a Black teen at the hands of police in San Francisco,

MEET TOMMIE SMITH AND JOHN CARLOS

The Black Power movement made an appearance at the 1968 Olympics. Tommie Smith and John Carlos placed in the 200-meter race. Smith won first place and Carlos placed third. As they stood on the podium to accept their awards, they both did something remarkable. They raised their fists as a symbol of the Black Power movement. They were banned from ever attending the Olympics again.

they felt it was time to act. In October 1966, they formed the Black Panther Party for Self-Defense. The Panthers pledged to monitor police activities in Black communities across the nation. Soon they gained support in major cities like Los Angeles, Chicago, and Philadelphia. By 1968, they had more than 2,000 members.

As the Black Panther Party grew, some leaders from the nonviolent movement took interest. On April 4, 1968, Martin Luther King Jr. was assassinated. It was a major blow to the movement. Without a strong leader, younger members turned to the new progressive movement. Stokely Carmichael was a Freedom Rider and a leader in the SNCC. He wanted to create something different for the movement. Carmichael saw an opportunity one day after a protest. He held a rally that was a call for Black people to unite and recognize their heritage. He used the term "Black Power" as a way to give power to people who had been treated poorly.

"Black Power" became the slogan for a generation. Soon Carmichael joined the growing Black Panther Party. But the popularity of the party caught the attention of the FBI. Led by J. Edgar Hoover, the FBI followed members of the party and even managed to split it up. The Black Panther Party eventually disbanded, but not without leaving its mark on American history.

THE BLACK ARTS MOVEMENT

As politics and culture changed, Black artists began to create something new. After the assassination of Malcolm X, Amiri Baraka created the Black Arts Repertory Theatre/School. Baraka was a poet who wrote about politics and Black unity. Here, Baraka and other Black artists created a new form of expression that rejected tradition. Soon the movement spread to areas across the nation. The art celebrated Black culture and encouraged Black pride. Some of the best-known artists of this time were Ntozake Shange, Maya Angelou, and James Baldwin.

Activist Angela Davis

The Trial of Angela Davis: 1970

Angela Davis was a young woman from segregated Alabama. She had joined the Black Panther Party and a branch of the Communist Party early on. She was also a professor. During this time, Davis was a vocal supporter of the Soledad brothers. The men were not actually brothers, but rather three African-American men accused of killing a prison guard. Many people across the nation thought they were innocent. It was a very controversial case. During their trial, Jonathan Jackson, the brother of one of the accused men, tried to free his brother. Unfortunately, the escape attempt ended in a shootout. The judge, two inmates, and Jackson were killed.

After an investigation, it was discovered that the guns Jackson used were registered in Angela Davis's name. Davis was charged in connection with the crime. She hid and was soon on the FBI's Most Wanted list. She was only the third woman ever to appear on that list. Davis was arrested in New York and had to go to trial. Some people thought Davis was guilty because she was outspoken about prison reform, which is a plan to improve conditions inside of prisons and find alternatives to sending people to prison. She was also friends with George Jackson, one

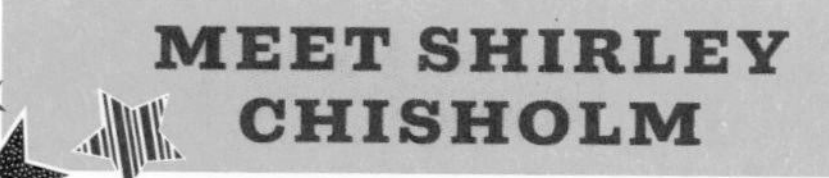

MEET SHIRLEY CHISHOLM

In 1968, four years before Angela Davis went to trial, Shirley Chisholm made history for Black women. Chisholm became the first African-American woman elected to the US House of Representatives. She had started her career in local politics in Brooklyn, New York. In 1972, Chisholm made history again by running for president. No Black person had ever run for president. She focused on racial equality and women's rights. Chisholm didn't win, but she made an impact on voters. Her fight for justice opened doors for other women of color in politics.

of the Soledad brothers. Aside from her friendship with George and the registered guns, however, there was little evidence to prove she was involved.

In March 1972, Davis went to trial. She had been in jail for more than a year. The case received national attention. A few months later, Davis was acquitted, or found not guilty, of all charges. She was a free woman. The trial made Davis more famous as an activist. She became the face of prison reform. She went on to talk and write about abolishing prisons. Her writings were important in the years to come.

ESSENCE MAGAZINE

As Black women began to have a voice in politics and culture, a new medium was created to reach this powerful group. *Essence* magazine began publishing in 1970. It was the first lifestyle magazine directed at Black women. The magazine quickly became popular. Black women were able to find articles about issues that were important to them. The magazine also featured Black models, like Beverly Johnson, who were not on the covers of white magazines.

Attorney General Robert Kennedy addressing civil rights demonstrators

The *Bakke* Decision and Affirmative Action: 1978

The phrase **affirmative action** was first used back in 1961, when President Kennedy ordered companies to take "affirmative action" to make sure they were using fair hiring practices. That meant employers had to make room for groups they had previously discriminated against, like African-Americans. Affirmative action was needed to help balance the playing field after years of discrimination. Otherwise, African-Americans would always be behind through no fault of their own. Soon affirmative action was used in education, too.

MEET ANDREW YOUNG

Andrew Young was a leader in the civil rights movement. He worked with Dr. King and other leaders for protests in Selma, Birmingham, and more. After King's death, Young went on to enter politics. He became a Congress member in Georgia. In 1977, the year before the *Bakke* decision, Young was appointed to serve as the US ambassador to the United Nations. He was the first African-American to hold this position.

Universities and colleges used different methods to determine who they admitted. Many had not been open to **minorities** before integration. They tried to find ways to increase the minority population in each school. The medical school at University of California, Davis, which admitted only 100 students per year, reserved 16 spots for minorities for each entering class. Allan Bakke was a white former Marine officer who wanted to attend medical school at UC Davis. He was rejected twice and filed a lawsuit against the school. He wanted to challenge their affirmative action policies. The case gained national attention. The California Supreme Court ruled in his favor. They ruled that the program violated the rights of white applicants.

UC Davis took the case to the US Supreme Court. The justices had a hard time making a decision, but ultimately they ruled in Bakke's favor. The court agreed that minorities should receive a fair shot. They also agreed that diversity in the classroom was important. But they stated that a person's race could not be the only reason they were admitted to a school. By the end, Bakke was admitted. The ruling was important in determining how affirmative action would work in education. Schools had to provide opportunity for those they had previously discriminated against, but they could not admit a person just because of the color of their skin. As the Seventies drew to an end, affirmative action would be an ongoing issue for the next generations.

ALEX HALEY'S *ROOTS*

The Black Arts Movement had created more interest in Black history. Alex Haley was an author who had studied his family's history from the time of the transatlantic slave trade. His book *Roots* was an instant hit. In 1977, Haley's family saga aired on national TV. For eight nights, America tuned in to the first televised drama of African-American history.

CHAPTER FIVE

1981 TO 2000

As African-Americans moved closer to the 21st century, America seemed to be a different place. The civil rights movement had taken place nearly 20 years earlier. Black people were in the same workplaces and schools as their white peers. It seemed America had finally rid itself of the ugliness of its past. The Black Power movement had given birth to a new generation of music, arts, and culture. A new style of music would soon take the world by storm. Black artists would take ownership of their own music labels just like Berry Gordy Jr. did for Motown. But even as Black people excelled, bias and racism were still very much a part of American life.

A prison in Massachusetts

The Rise of Mass Incarceration: 1980s

Crime rates began to boom around the late Seventies. As the new decade began, America saw more Black people put in jail or prison than ever before. Politicians began promising tough crime **reform** to gain supporters. These laws unfairly targeted minority communities. They also created longer sentences for small crimes. The African-American community wanted change. Leaders like Jesse Jackson and the NAACP called on communities to come together. They knew it was a new fight for Black people to be treated fairly in the court systems. Meanwhile, the effects of mass incarceration were seen in Black communities across the nation.

Some communities developed a distrust of the legal system. In large cities like New York and Los Angeles, racial tension was brewing. Communities of color were being targeted by the local police. Mass incarceration also saw many Black men separated from their families. Stories of mistreatment spread through a new form of music. Young African-Americans started rhyming to beats. Their rhymes talked about their lives and the violence in their communities. At first, this new type of music was strictly underground. It was not popular at all. As the violence and crime in the communities got worse,

MEET DIANA ROSS

Diana Ross was born and raised in Detroit. She gained fame as the lead singer for the chart-topping girl group The Supremes. The Supremes brought worldwide attention to the Motown sound. Ross was one of the most popular acts on Gordy's Motown Records. She starred in movies, even earning an Academy Award nomination. Today, Ross is known for earning the Female Entertainer of the Century award. Her contributions to the popularity and success of African-American music were groundbreaking.

however, the music found an audience outside the community. People all over the nation heard about police mistreatment. They also heard about the poverty and crime in certain communities. It was time to take the message to the mainstream. For some, music became a new way to fight the power.

CAROL MOSELEY BRAUN

As racist policies continued to affect African-American communities throughout the Eighties, representatives fought for fair treatment. One of those fighters was Carol Moseley Braun. For years, Moseley Braun was a member of the Illinois House of Representatives. She fought against the death penalty and promoted equality. She went on to become the first African-American woman to serve as US senator and only the second Black senator since the Reconstruction era.

Def Jam artist LL Cool J

Founding of Def Jam Recordings: 1983

Black artists continued to pave their own way in the Eighties. Def Jam Recordings was formed by Rick Rubin and Russell Simmons. Simmons was already known in the music industry and soon became the face of a new music style called hip-hop. Once the two got together, Def Jam became home to some of the most popular hip-hop artists. But Def Jam was not just another record label. Def Jam was also responsible for moving hip-hop music into the mainstream. Before, hip-hop artists were not well known. Hip-hop was mostly popular in Black communities. The first record

Def Jam created was by a Black artist named LL Cool J. Soon they released music by a white rap group, Beastie Boys. Def Jam wanted to produce good music, regardless of the artist's race, and increase hip-hop's popularity.

Soon Def Jam signed more controversial artists whose music spoke about life in poor and underserved neighborhoods. They rapped about life, love, and loss in their communities. These songs became popular for showing a side of America that was not pretty or publicized. This style of music soon took over the radio. By the end of the decade, rap music, or hip-hop, was everywhere. It seemed that

MEET THE SUGARHILL GANG

Before Def Jam released its first hip-hop records, The Sugarhill Gang made history for their song "Rapper's Delight." The Sugarhill Gang was a rap trio from New Jersey. In the late Seventies, the trio was influenced by the underground style of rhyming and rapping. The young members were brought together by a music producer. Michael, Henry, and Guy soon began rapping together. Their first song went on to be the first rap single to appear on the *Billboard* Hot 100. Their early success in bringing hip-hop to the mainstream was influential on Def Jam.

everyone wanted to profit from the stories of poor communities. As the label grew, so did its roster of artists. Jay-Z, DMX, and Kanye West contributed to the major success of the label. Def Jam's early impact was historic.

1989 BEST RAP PERFORMANCE

Rap music was reluctantly accepted in the mainstream. In 1989, the Grammy Awards added a category for the booming new type of music. Each year the Grammys picked the best artists in each music category. But they didn't want to televise the rap category. Will Smith and other artists boycotted the ceremony. The winner was called. DJ Jazzy Jeff and the Fresh Prince won for their song "Parents Just Don't Understand." The Fresh Prince, also known as Will Smith, did not accept the award, but his partner did. Smith went on to become one of the biggest stars in the world. Once an underground art form, rap music was set to take over the airways.

Jesse Jackson campaigning for president

Jesse Jackson and Voter Registration: 1984

African-Americans had achieved much, but many felt that President Ronald Reagan's policies were not helpful to their communities. Reagan had cut taxes on the wealthy and broadened the War on Drugs. He created harsher laws that harmed minorities. It was time for a Black presidential candidate. Jesse Jackson heard the call and launched a national campaign. Jackson was an activist who had worked closely with Martin Luther King Jr. during the civil rights movement. After King's death, Jackson led the SCLC. He eventually created his own organization to face injustice. Jackson ran as a Democrat and set his goal to become the first Black president. Years earlier, Shirley Chisholm had the same goal. She was the first African-American to have a nationwide campaign for president of the United States.

In 1984, Jackson began his campaign. Many people didn't take him seriously. His own party members thought he was wasting his time. But he surprised everyone when he took third place overall. How did he do it? Jackson's campaign focused on getting more Black voters. He had voter registration drives that increased the Black turnout in many states. In some states, like New Jersey, he tripled the Black voter turnout! Jackson became the first African-American candidate to win a major state

MEET THE NATIONAL RAINBOW COALITION

The National Rainbow Coalition was a political organization started out of Jesse Jackson's presidential campaign. He called for all groups that had been overlooked to join Black and Jewish Americans. He thought that together they could push for change. The coalition eventually merged with People United to Save Humanity (PUSH). PUSH was another of Jackson's organizations. By merging the organizations, Jackson hoped to build enough national support to demand fair treatment and equality for all.

primary. Just 20 years after the March on Washington, a Black person had made a major impact in a presidential race.

BLACK ENTERTAINMENT TELEVISION

During the Eighties, music videos were very popular. MTV aired the newest music videos from popular artists. But many Black artists were not shown on MTV. Entrepreneur Robert Johnson had created Black Entertainment Television (BET) the year before MTV launched. He formed partnerships with record labels and gained popularity. Black music artists were welcome at BET. The new station became a hit. Soon MTV began playing Black music videos. BET opened the doors for Black musicians to be seen all over the world.

LA residents protest police violence after Rodney King is beaten

Los Angeles Riots: 1992

In the Nineties, incarceration rates of Black people were still on the rise. Black communities across America were on edge. In Los Angeles, Black community leaders complained about the **excessive force** used by the Los Angeles Police Department. On March 3, 1991, an unarmed man named Rodney King was beaten by several police officers. The beating was caught on camera and sent to the local news. The nation watched in horror as King was beaten for nearly 20 minutes. The Black community was angry. It had complained about the harsh treatment for years. Soon charges were brought against the officers. A trial date was set.

MEET TONI MORRISON

The Nineties was a period of racial unrest, but also Black literary achievement. In 1993, Toni Morrison became the first African-American to win the Nobel Prize in Literature. Morrison had been one of the first Black editors at a major publisher and helped bring books by other Black authors into the mainstream. Morrison won many awards, including a Pulitzer. Her writing features Black women and centers Black culture. Some of her books include *The Bluest Eye*, *Song of Solomon*, and *Beloved*.

Meanwhile, tension between Black communities and local Korean business owners was growing. On March 16, 1991, a Black teenager named Latasha Harlins was killed by a Korean store owner. The store owner thought she was stealing orange juice. After Harlins's death, police found she had not been stealing. The community wanted justice. The store owner only did community service and paid a fine.

A year later, on April 29, 1992, a jury acquitted all officers involved in the King beating. The Black community felt like there was no justice for Harlins, and none for King. That day, riots started in different locations around Los Angeles. Soon they spread to the whole city. Rioters looted stores, attacked people, and burned businesses. The rioters also destroyed Koreatown.

It took three days for the major rioting to stop. Rodney King gave a speech asking everyone to "get along." By the fourth day, thousands of federal troops arrived to control the chaos. On the fifth day, the mayor assured everyone that things were under control. But acts of violence continued for days afterward. The LA riots changed America. These protesters were not peaceful. They were angry rioters who had taken things into their own hands. Community leaders knew that race relations in Los Angeles needed time to heal.

MAYA ANGELOU

Maya Angelou was a writer, poet, and creative. Her most popular works stem from the Black Arts Movement of the Seventies. Angelou became a prominent speaker during the early Nineties. She recited a poem at the inauguration of President Bill Clinton in January 1993. Angelou is one of the most celebrated Black poets and activists in modern times. She went on to inspire Black pride in a new generation fueled by the power of words.

Marchers at the Million Man March

Million Man March: 1995

As the Nineties moved forward, the Nation of Islam came back to the forefront. Louis Farrakhan was now the leader of the group. Farrakhan was a controversial speaker. He preached in support of Black power, but also segregation. He wanted Black people to deal with their communities separately. He also said negative things about other minority groups. His goals were not aligned with what the civil rights movement had fought for, but he planned to unite Black people across America. He wanted to give Black people hope amid the ongoing violence, high unemployment rates, and mass incarceration. He also wanted to improve the media image of Black men. He called for one million Black men to meet in Washington, DC, for the largest march in American history. His goal was to have a day of unity and hope.

Some Black leaders did not support the march. John Lewis, who was now a Georgia senator, did not. Coretta Scott King, Martin Luther King Jr.'s widow, did not support it either. They thought Farrakhan's message would divide America. Jesse Jackson and the NAACP, however, supported the march. On October 16, 1995, thousands of Black

MEET DR. BETTY SHABAZZ

In 1965, Shabazz became the widow of Malcolm X. Left with six young daughters to raise, Shabazz kept away from the spotlight. After witnessing her husband's assassination, she had nightmares and did not want to deal with the unfairness of what happened to Malcolm. Eventually Shabazz became a speaker. She talked about Malcolm, but she discussed her own life as well. She enrolled in college, got her doctorate degree, and eventually worked at Medgar Evers College in Brooklyn. Despite her rocky relationship with the Nation of Islam, she spoke at the Million Man March. Shabazz, Myrlie Evers-Williams, and Coretta Scott King kept their husbands' legacy alive while forging their own way with volunteer work and activism.

men from across the nation met in Washington, DC. The day was filled with positive messages about unity and family. It was reported that nearly 600,000 men attended. The media covered the event, with special guests Maya Angelou and Dr. Betty Shabazz, the widow of Malcolm X. Overall, it was a positive event. The success of the Million Man March showed that there was still something worth marching for. The times had changed, but ideas of Black power and unity continued to be important. It also showed that Black men were concerned about their families. They met to show the world that they wanted unity and a better life.

A MILLION WOMEN

As an answer to the Million Man March, a women's march was planned to be held in Philadelphia in 1997. The major themes of the march were family unity and issues specific to Black women. This march called for Black women to unify. Women from different cultures and backgrounds supported the march. Soon it became a call to unite Black women across the globe. The march went on to become one of the largest gatherings of women in America.

Senator Barack Obama

Barack Obama Elected to the Illinois Senate: 1996

As the nation edged closer to the 21st century, in Illinois, a young Black lawyer was on his way to change history. Barack Obama was elected to the Illinois state Senate in 1996. Obama was a different type of politician. He did not come from wealth. He also was known for leading community organizations in Chicago. There he helped set up job training programs and tutoring. He had even worked as a civil rights attorney. As a new senator, he represented the South Side of Chicago, which was the same area he had helped as a community organizer.

MEET KAMALA HARRIS

As Barack Obama was making his path to the White House, a young Kamala Harris was well on her way, too. In 1998, Harris became the managing attorney of the Career Criminal Unit of the San Francisco District Attorney's Office. She soon went on to win the election for district attorney. Although some people disagreed with her policies, she had a deep commitment to justice. Soon Harris became the attorney general for the state of California. In 2020, Harris made history as the first woman of color to become vice president.

In 1998, Obama was reelected to the Illinois Senate. He was also becoming more popular. He worked with Democrats and Republicans to create better health care laws. He also wrote a law that helped low-income workers. These workers had a hard time affording housing and electricity. Obama tried to give them a few breaks to prevent them from becoming homeless. During the last years of the century, Obama set his sights on making history as the first Black president. He went on to become a US senator and then the president of the United States. Obama was proof that change was possible.

SOUTH SIDE, CHICAGO

During the Great Migration, many Black Southerners fled to Chicago. They created businesses and a vibrant community in the South Side. The area was segregated. During the Sixties a new highway was built that acted as a racial divide—Black people on one side and white people on the other. When segregation legally ended, affordable housing was built only on the South Side. The South Side became known as a low-income area. And in some neighborhoods, violence took over. Community leaders like Obama led efforts to improve the area and grant its residents more equality.

LOOKING AHEAD

The 20th century was a turning point for America. It was a time when African-Americans had to find their place in a country that had treated them as property for hundreds of years. Through every decade, Black people endured hardships. It's important for us to understand how African-Americans persevered through those hard times, and why past trauma may affect how African-Americans deal with certain issues today. Just as we learn and understand the hard times, it is important to celebrate the good. African-Americans have influenced culture through sports, art, science, and music. As a community, they've also influenced politics. The civil rights movement was a win not just for African-Americans but for other minorities as well. Protests and marches set the stage for all groups to fight for equal rights. These groups included women and the LGBTQ community. The civil rights movement opened the doors for all groups that had previously been left out or suffered discrimination.

African-American history also shows us how history links to the present. The protests of the past made way for new forms of protest, like the Black Lives Matter movement. The new movement demanded accountability and justice for violence and brutality against African-Americans. This movement stated that Black lives could not be ignored. The 21st century brought in a new era of leaders and culture. America voted for the first African-American president, and in 2020, the nation welcomed its first woman of color vice president. There was also a culture of Black excellence and progress that promised to keep moving forward. The sacrifices of the past made way for Black people to succeed today. As the nation keeps improving, it's important to look at history to make sure we don't repeat the mistakes of the past. More than 100 years ago, the United States was a mostly segregated nation. Today, we enjoy a diverse nation that is full of hope and progress.

GLOSSARY

Affirmative action: An effort to actively improve employment or educational opportunities for minorities

Appeal: When a case is brought before a higher court to review the decision made by a lower court

Assimilate: To join in the traditions of a population or group

Black nationalists: African-Americans who promote Black empowerment and resist integration

Black Pride: An African-American movement or feeling of pride in their history and achievements

Civil Rights Act of 1964: This act made it illegal to discriminate against people based on their color, race, religion, sex, or nationality

Civil rights movement: A campaign created by African-Americans and allies to end racial segregation and discrimination

Demonstration: A public display of a group's concerns or feelings toward a cause

Discriminate: To treat someone differently or unfairly based on the color of their skin

Emancipation Proclamation: An order made by President Abraham Lincoln to free enslaved people in Southern states. Although the order was meant to immediately end slavery, some states took more than a year to officially do so.

Excessive force: Force used beyond what is reasonable or necessary

Fraternity: A men's organization formed for social purposes

The Great Depression: A 10-year period of economic depression that began in the United States in the 1930s and spread internationally

The Great Migration: The time between 1916 and the late 1960s when Southern African-Americans moved north for better opportunities and to escape Jim Crow laws

Hate crime: A violent crime motivated by prejudice

Integration: Bringing people together as equals, regardless of their skin color

Jim Crow: The name given to Southern segregation laws

Minority: A group of people that are fewer in number than the majority

Pan-Africanism: An international movement that encourages unity among all people of African descent

Racism: Unfairness, injustice, and harm perpetrated by a dominant or powerful group against another group because of the color of their skin

Reform: To amend or improve a system that isn't working

Renaissance: A time period of great artistic and intellectual activity

Segregation: The practice of keeping people separate based on their skin color

Sharecropping: Mostly Southern African-Americans, sharecroppers farmed small plots of land in exchange for shelter and a share of the crop. This practice often kept Black families in poverty and indebted to the landowner.

Vigilante justice: When someone takes it upon themselves to right a perceived wrong

Voting Rights Act of 1965: This act made it illegal to use literacy tests or discriminate against African-American voters

White supremacy: The false belief that white people are better than or superior to any other race of people, and that they have the right to oppress other people

RESOURCES

Places to Visit

The King Center in Atlanta, Georgia

National Museum of African American History in Washington, DC.

National Underground Railroad Freedom Center in Cincinnati, Ohio

Whitney Plantation in Wallace, Louisiana

Books

Brown v. Board of Education: A Day That Changed America by Margeaux Weston

The March on Washington: A Day That Changed America by Margeaux Weston

100 African-Americans Who Shaped American History by Chrisanne Beckner

Civil Rights Then and Now: A Timeline of the Fight for Equality in America by Kristina Daniele

Websites

PBS.org

CivilRightsTrail.com

SELECTED REFERENCES

American Association for Access, Equity, and Diversity. "More History of Affirmative Action Policies from the 1960s." Accessed April 24, 2021. aaaed.org/aaaed/history_of_affirmative_action.asp

Duncan, Garrett Albert. "Black Panther Party." *Britannica*. Last updated February 9, 2021. britannica.com/topic/Black-Panther-Party/additional-info#history

The Editors of Encyclopaedia Britannica. "Montgomery Bus Boycott." *Britannica*. Last updated November 28, 2020. britannica.com/event/Montgomery-bus-boycott

History.com Editors. "Brown v. Board of Education of Topeka." HISTORY. Last updated January 19, 2021. history.com/topics/black-history/brown-v-board-of-education-of-topeka

Hutchinson, George. "Harlem Renaissance." *Britannica*. Last updated March 17, 2021. britannica.com/event/Harlem-Renaissance-American-literature-and-art

Klein, Christopher. "How Selma's 'Bloody Sunday' Became a Turning Point in the Civil Rights Movement." HISTORY. Last updated July 18, 2020. history.com/news/selma-bloody-sunday-attack-civil-rights-movement

Maranzani, Barbara. "Behind Martin Luther King's Searing 'Letter from a Birmingham Jail'." HISTORY. Last updated August 31, 2018. history.com/news/kings-letter-from-birmingham-jail-50-years-later

Nix, Elizabeth. "Tuskegee Experiment: The Infamous Syphilis Study." HISTORY. Last updated December 15, 2020. history.com/news/the-infamous-40-year-tuskegee-study

Woodward, Laurie. "Brotherhood of Sleeping Car Porters." *Britannica*. Last updated April 12, 2016. britannica.com/topic/Brotherhood-of-Sleeping-Car-Porters

ACKNOWLEDGMENTS

This book would not have been possible without the support of my best friend, accountability partner, and husband, Jarod. Thank you for your encouragement and selfless care. I'd also like to thank my editor, Eliza. You made writing this so much easier through your help and understanding. To my wonderful, smart, beautiful brown sons, thank you for being my sunshine every day. I cannot wait to witness the amazing things you will achieve. Lastly, to the African-Americans who came before me, thank you for all that you are and the legacy you left behind.

ABOUT THE AUTHOR

Margeaux Weston is an editor, sensitivity reader, and writer. She holds an English degree, with a concentration in writing and culture, from Louisiana State University. She has written four children's books and edited many more. Margeaux is also an editor at the Hugo-nominated *Fiyah Magazine*. As an editor, she enjoys working on speculative fiction, kid lit, nonfiction, and historical fiction.